Hair Braiding and Friendship Bracelets

p

This is a Parragon book
This edition published in 2005

Parragon
Queen Street House
4 Queen Street
Bath BA1 1HE

Written and Produced by
Caroline Repchuk
Art: Heather Heyworth
Photography: David Ellwand
Hairstyling: Christine Taylor
Friendship Bracelets: Claire Keen

Printed and bound in China
ISBN 1-40545-865-8

1ntroduction

This guide to braiding gives you the know-how to make amazing friendship bracelets, and create fabulous looks with beads and braids for your hair.

Step-by-step instructions will show you how to make some fantastic bracelets to wear, or to give to your friends and family! And you can use the same techniques to create some cool accessories to use in the fabulous braided hairstyles.

So hold out your hand in friendship, grab your best bud and have fun!

Remember to keep all beads and small parts out of the reach of babies and small children.

Contents

Friendship Bracelets

If you keep your equipment ready in a box, you can make friendship bracelets almost anywhere!

You Will Need: Scissors A Ruler Sticky Tape
A Clipboard – this is a good, portable surface to work on.
You could use a piece of thick card with a bulldog clip at the top.
Thread – inexpensive to buy from sewing departments.
Beads – available at craft or bead shops.

The Basic Knot

You need to learn to tie this knot in two directions, to make many of the bracelets in this book.

Left-Loop

1. Knot two threads together and clip or tape them to your board. Hold thread B tightly. Cross thread A over thread B, leaving a loop sticking out.

2. Pass thread A under thread B and through the loop. Gently pull it to make a knot. Slide the knot to the top and pull it tight.

3. Repeat so you have a double knot. This is a complete left-loop knot.

Right-Loop

1. Hold thread B tightly. Cross thread A over thread B, leaving a loop sticking out.

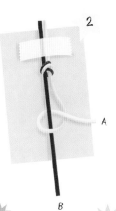

2. Pass thread A under thread B and through the loop. Gently pull it to make a knot. Slide the knot to the top and pull tight.

3. Repeat so you have a complete right-loop knot.

Hot Hints

Wrap a string around the wrist or ankle of the person your bracelet is for, and cut to size. Use as a guide so you know how long to make the bracelet.

Twister

This cool bracelet is the easiest to make – so get twistin'!
Choose three colours and cut three threads, 60cm long.

1. Tie a knot 7cm from the top, and tape the
threads to your board. Electrical tape from
hardware stores works well.

2. Hold the threads together
and, pulling firmly, twist them
until they feel tight.

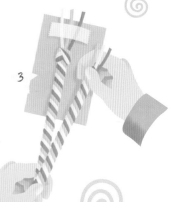

3

3. Hold the twist firm with one
hand, and put a finger from your
other hand in the middle.
Now fold it in half, so
the ends meet.

Hot Hints
It's a good idea to use three different colours to
start, as it makes the instructions easier to follow.
Once you feel confident, you can let your imagination
run wild, creating any colour combination you like.

10

4. Hold the ends firmly. Remove your finger, and the twisted threads will quickly wind together, leaving a loop at one end.

5. Take the tape off and tie a knot in the free ends at the right length. Pull the knot through the loop to fasten. Hold the bracelet tight while you tie the knot or it will unwind.

Well done! You've made your first bracelet!

Hot Hints
Make a thicker bracelet by using more threads.
Add a large bead by pushing it over the looped end.

11

Easy-Peasy Plaits

This bracelet is so quick and easy, you can make one to match every outfit! Choose three colours and cut three lengths of each colour, about 40cm long.

1. Knot the threads at one end, and clip or tape them to your board.

A
B
C

2. Separate the colours, and spread them out in strands. Take strand C and cross it over strand B. Strand C is now in the middle.

A   C   B

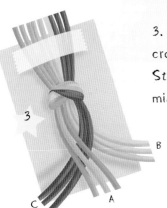

3. Now take strand A and cross it over strand C. Strand A is now in the middle.

4. Continue plaiting in the same way, right over middle, left over middle, until the bracelet is long enough.
Tie the ends in a knot, then fasten it on to your wrist.

Hot Hints
As it is so quick and easy, this is a good pattern to choose if you want to make a long braid to wear as a headband, or around your belly.

13

✳ Simple Stripes ✳

This uses the basic left-loop knot, and is perfect for beginners! Choose three colours that blend or contrast well. Cut two lengths 70cm long of each colour.

1. Knot the six threads 7cm from the top. Clip or tape them to your board. Lay them out as shown.

A B

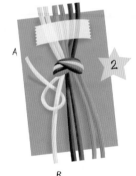

A

2

B

2. Start with thread A, and make a left-loop knot on thread B, following the instructions on page 8. Remember to tie a double knot each time!

Hot Hints
Add beads by threading them on before the first or last knot of a row. Use the colour of the stripes to help you space the beads evenly.

14

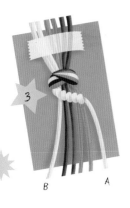

3. Using thread A, continue making left-loop knots over each thread, until you reach the end of the row. Leave thread A on the right-hand side.

B   A

4. Now take thread B, and make left-loop knots over each thread across the row.

A   B

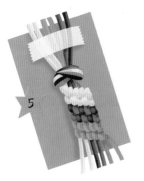

5. Keep going, using each thread in turn, to make a pattern of repeating diagonal stripes.

6. When the bracelet is long enough, tie the ends together in a knot, and trim them neatly with scissors.

15

Cupid's Arrow

Make this bracelet for someone you love! This pattern uses both left and right-hand knots. Choose four colours, and cut two threads in each colour, 70cm long.

1. Knot the threads 7cm from the top. Clip or tape them to your board. Lay them out as shown.

A B C D E F G H

2. Use thread A to make a left-loop knot on threads B, C and D, following the instructions on page 8. Leave thread A in the middle.

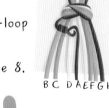

B C D A E F G H

3. Now take thread H and make right-loop knots on threads G, F and E, leaving thread H in the middle.

B C D A H E F G

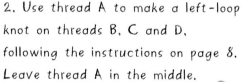

16

4. Knot thread A and thread H together, using either a left or right-loop knot. This makes the point of the arrow.

B C D H A E F G

5

A B C D E F G H

5. Repeat from step 2 using the new outside threads, and knotting into the middle. After four rows the threads will be back in their original position.

6. When the bracelet is long enough, finish it by tying a knot and plaiting the ends.

Hot Hints
Add beads by threading them on to the outside strand you are about to knot with. Make sure you have enough beads to complete your bracelet before you start.

Zig Zag

The fantastic zig zag shape of this bracelet is simply made by alternating knotting from left to right, and right to left! Choose four colours, and cut eight threads, each 90cm long.

Hot Hints
Add a bead
to accentuate
each point.

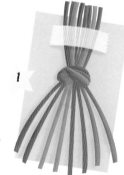

1

1. Knot your threads 7cm from the top, clip or tape them to your board. Lay out the pairs of colours, as shown.

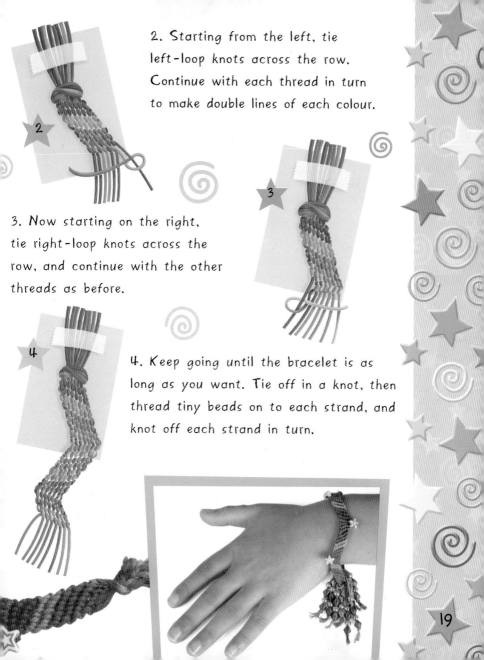

2. Starting from the left, tie left-loop knots across the row. Continue with each thread in turn to make double lines of each colour.

3. Now starting on the right, tie right-loop knots across the row, and continue with the other threads as before.

4. Keep going until the bracelet is as long as you want. Tie off in a knot, then thread tiny beads on to each strand, and knot off each strand in turn.

19

Mermaids' Beads

This swirly bracelet has a spiral of knots running down it which look like beads. It looks fantastic – and it's very easy to make! You will need six threads in different colours, each 60cm long.

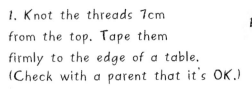

1. Knot the threads 7cm from the top. Tape them firmly to the edge of a table. (Check with a parent that it's OK.)

2. Take one thread and hold the other five together in one strand. Make a left-loop knot over the other threads together and pull it up tightly.

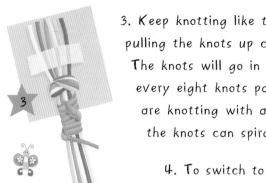

3. Keep knotting like this for 1 or 2cm, pulling the knots up close together. The knots will go in a spiral. After every eight knots pass the thread you are knotting with around the back so the knots can spiral properly.

4. To switch to another colour, take out another thread close to the last knot you made. Put the old thread with the others, and continue knotting with the new thread. Use each colour in turn, and repeat to form a pattern.

5. When the bracelet is long enough, finish it by knotting and plaiting the ends.

Hot Hints
This braid looks very pretty if you make it long enough to wear around your belly. Add beads to the bracelet before tying a knot, and do the next knot quite loosely.

21

Broken Ladder

This beautiful bracelet looks complicated, but if you've tried making the Cupid's Arrow and Mermaids' Beads patterns, you will not find it too hard, as it combines the two!

Choose four colours. Cut two threads of each, 70cm long.

1. Knot the threads 7cm from the top and clip or tape them to your board. Lay them out as shown.

2. Following the instructions on pages 16 and 17, knot the threads in the arrow pattern until you have used each colour. The threads will be back in the order you started with.

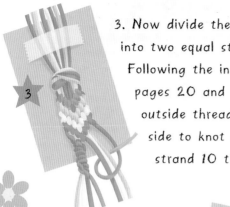

3. Now divide the threads into two equal strands. Following the instructions on pages 20 and 21, use the outside thread from each side to knot around each strand 10 times.

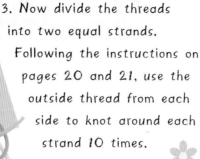

4. Lay out the threads again as shown. The outside threads you used to knot around the strands should now be in the middle. Repeat the arrow pattern, again using each colour.

5. Continue alternating the two patterns until the bracelet is long enough, then finish by knotting the ends.

Hot Hints
Practise the Cupid's Arrow and Mermaids' Beads patterns before trying this bracelet.

Going Loopy

Just two colours are needed to make this pretty bracelet. You will need four lengths 30cm long for the middle colour, and four threads 60cm long to tie in loopy knots around the outside.

Hot Hints
This braid looks best when you use a dark colour for the middle threads, and a lighter colour for the outside ones.

1. Knot the threads and clip or tape them to your board. Lay them out with the shorter threads in the middle, and a pair of the longer threads on each side, which you will work with as one strand.

2. Take strand A, and cross it over the middle threads, leaving a loop on the left. Pass strand A under strand B.

3. Now pass strand B under strand A and the middle threads, pull it through the loop on the left, and over strand A. Slide the knot to the top.

24

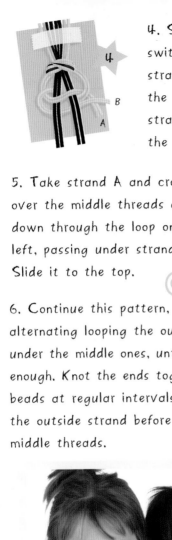

4. Strand A and B have switched sides. Take strand B, and pass it under the middle threads and over strand A, leaving a loop on the left side.

5. Take strand A and cross it over the middle threads and down through the loop on the left, passing under strand B. Slide it to the top.

6. Continue this pattern, alternating looping the outside threads over and under the middle ones, until the braid is long enough. Knot the ends together to finish. Add beads at regular intervals by slipping them onto the outside strand before crossing it over the middle threads.

25

Starry Night

Follow the instructions carefully, and this twinkling pattern is not as hard as it looks! Cut four lengths of one colour, 90cm long. Cut two lengths of two other colours, 80cm long.

1. Knot the threads, clip or tape them to your board, and lay them out as shown.

ABCD EFGH

2. Following the instructions on pages 16 and 17, tie left and right-loop knots to form an arrow pattern, until you have four rows.

A B C D E F G H

3. Use thread A to make a left-loop knot on thread B. Use thread H to make a right-loop knot on thread G.

A B   G H

Hot Hints
Slip the thread onto a large needle, to make it easier to slide the beads on.

26

4. Using the middle threads, knot the right one over all the threads to the right, using left-loop knots. Use the left one to knot all the threads to the left, using right-loop knots.

D AB CFGH E

5. Knot the new middle threads together. Repeat step 4, working out from the middle, until you have completed four rows, and the threads are back in their original position.

A BCD EFG H

6. Knot the middle threads together. Knot the right middle thread over the next thread, using a left-loop knot. Knot the left middle thread over the next thread, using a right-loop knot. Knot the new middle threads together. The two middle colours have now switched over.

AB DCFEGH

7. Continue following steps 2–6 until the bracelet is long enough. Tie a knot, add a small bead to each thread, and tie off.

Take Care of Your Hair

Lustrous locks need love and attention, so whether your hair's long or short, straight or curly, blonde or brunette, give it the TLC it deserves!

Washing your hair too often strips it of its natural oils. Use a product suited to your hair type, and switch brands from time to time, to prevent build-up on your hair.

Most styles are easier to do and look better on hair that has been washed a day or two before.
Your hair will grow longer and stronger if it is trimmed regulary - every 6 weeks if possible!
Don't use a brush on wet hair, or you could damage it.
Comb it through, gently removing any tangles by holding your hair at the roots, and working up from the ends.

Adding Beads

Here's how to add beads to some of the plaited styles that follow:

You will need beads, a hair threader and bead stoppers, all available from high street stores.

1. Secure the end of a small plait with a hair grip. Place your beads on to a plastic hair threader.

2. Take off the hair grip, and pass the end of the plait through the loop of the threader.

3. Push the beads towards the plait, and pull on the threader, until the plait is pulled through the beads.

4. Push a bead stopper into the last bead.

Ponytail

A simple ponytail keeps your hair neat, tidy and off your face, and stops it from getting tangled. It also forms the basis of many other styles.

1. Brush your hair, removing any tangles by holding your hair at the roots, and brushing gently at the bottom

2. Put a hair band over your wrist, gather your hair together at the back of your head, and hold it in the hand with the band.

3. Using the other hand, slip the band off your wrist and over the ponytail.

4. Twist the band and pull the ponytail back through as many times as you need to, until the band is tight.

Flipover

For an extra twist, you can
flip your ponytail over using
a tool called a styler.

1. Gently push the pointed end into the
hair, above the middle of the band.

2. Thread your ponytail through the
loop, then pull the styler down, and
your ponytail will flip over. If your
hair is long enough, you could finish
it off with a plait, following the
instructions on pages 32 and 33.

Hot Hint
Never use elastic bands to
secure your hair as they
will damage it. Always use
proper hair bands or
scrunchies. Gather hair
together on the top of your
head for a high ponytail.
Make it even more dynamic
by securing it with several
bands or scrunchies.

Perfect Plaits

Once you get the hang of plaiting it's very easy. Plaits of different sizes can be used to create all kinds of funky styles!

1. Start by parting your hair down the centre. Using the hair on one side, divide it into three equal strands. Hold one outside section in each hand.

2. Cross the back strand over the middle strand, taking hold of it with the other hand, and using your fingers to keep the strands separate.

3. Now cross the front strand over the middle strand, passing it to the other hand, again using your fingers to keep the strands separate.

4. Continue plaiting, back to middle, front to middle, until you reach the end, then secure with a hair band. Repeat with the hair on the other side of your head.

Hot Hints
It may help to practise on a friend until you've got the hang of it!
Tie friendship braids around the hair bands for the look of a true Red Indian squaw!

Party Plaits

This style works best with long hair. It takes a while, so find a friend to help, or your arms may end up sore!

1. Brush your hair, and secure it with a hair band on the top of your head, in a high ponytail.

2. Divide your ponytail into six equal sections, held with hair grips.
Divide one section into three and plait it following the instructions on pages 32 and 33. Repeat with each strand.

3. Now hold five of the plaits in one hand, and wind the sixth plait around the base of the ponytail with your other. Secure it in place with hairpins.

4. Decorate the ends of your plaits with ribbons or beads. Get set to party!

Braid Parade

Small beaded braids look fantastic framing your face.

1. Make a straight parting with a comb across your head from ear to ear. Secure the back section of your hair in a high ponytail.

2. Make a centre parting in the front section of your hair and divide each

side into equal sections to plait around your face. Finish each plait with beads, following the instructions on page 29.

3. As an alternative to leaving all the braids hanging, you could sweep some up into your ponytail.

Hot Hints
Try to keep the beads on your braids at the same level. Choose coloured beads to match your outfit.

Hippy Chick

This groovy hairstyle is very easy, and a great way to show off your friendship braids!

1. Make a straight centre parting using a comb. Take a small section of hair from one side of your parting, plait it to the ends, and secure with a band. Repeat on the other side.

2. Take the plaits around to the back of your head, and secure them together with a hair band. Release the bands at the ends of the plaits, and unravel them up to the band at the top. Tie a friendship braid around to cover the band.

36

3. Plait two more sections of hair in front of each ear, and thread on beads, following the instructions on page 29.

Hot Hints
Short on time? Secure the top section of your hair in a ponytail and slip on a hippy headband!

Do the Twist

This simple style looks stunning. It works well with shorter hair too, so is great if your hair is not long enough to plait.

1. Using a comb, part your hair into six sections across the front of your head. Clip each section together.

2. Take one section and twist it round and round tightly, right to the roots, pulling it back as you do so. Secure the twist with a butterfly clip.

3. Repeat with the remaining sections, working across your head.

4. Jazz up with as many decorations as you like. Clip-on beads, like the ones used here, work really well attached to each twist.

Hot Hints
Wrap a Twister friendship braid around the spirals for an extra fashion twist in the tale!

Spinning Spirals

This works well with shoulder-length or longer hair, and looks fun whether your hair is straight or curly.

1. Divide your hair into three sections across the top of your head.

2. As before, twist your hair tightly until it starts to spiral. Eventually it will curl right around itself and into a tight knot.

3. Secure the knot with hair grips. Repeat with the other sections, then decorate with butterfly clips and sparkly hair accessories.

It's a Wrap

You'll need a friend
for this! Take it in
turns to do each
other's hair, and
soon you'll both
be turning heads!

1. Cut three lengths of different
coloured threads, twice the length
of the hair you are going to wrap.
Take a strand of hair, place it in
the middle of the threads and knot
them on tightly, close to the roots.

2. Hold the strand of hair away
from the head. Take one of the
threads and wind it tightly round
and round the hair and the other
threads as neatly as you can.

3. After a couple of centimetres, switch to another colour. Keep alternating the colours until you reach the end of the strand.

4. Add some beads at the bottom, and secure by tying off the threads in a knot.

Hot Hints
If you don't have time to wrap your hair, try pinning or clipping in some plaited friendship braids.

41

French Plait

French braids look so sleek and sophisticated, that it's worth taking time to practise, to get this style neat and tidy. For the best results, try and find someone to do it for you! Shoulder-length hair looks fantastic plaited down each side.

1. Make a straight centre parting using a comb. Starting at the front, divide your hair into three sections.

2. Plait left over middle, right over middle, as before.

3. Take up another loose section of hair from the left and add it to the left section as you plait it. Do the same on the right side.

4. Plait again, left over middle, right over middle. Stop to gather more hair into each outside strand and plait once more.

5. Keep plaiting over your ear and down the side of your head, gathering in more hair as you go.

6. By the time you reach the nape of your neck, all of your hair should have been gathered into the three strands. Continue plaiting to the ends and fasten with a hair band.

Hot Hints
Try adding some beaded hairpins for an even prettier finish to this style.

Braidy Bunch

These bouncy bunches will put a spring in your step!

1. Part your hair in the centre. Divide off small sections and plait them as before, securing the ends with small bands. You will not be plaiting all your hair, so hold the loose hair out of the way with a clip.

2. Gather together the loose hair and the braided hair on each side, and secure in two bunches.

3. Take one of the braids and wrap it around the base of each bunch, and secure it in place with hairpins. Finish by wrapping plaited friendship braids around the end of each plait, and tying off securely.

Racy Ribbons

Long straight hair will show off this style with the best effect, although it will still work on shorter braids.

1. Divide your hair into small sections and plait it all over. You may need some help at the back. Secure the ends with small hair bands.

2. Take a piece of soft, narrow ribbon more than twice the length of the braid and fold it in half. Tie it to the top of the plait. Bind down the length of the plait, crossing the ribbon alternately at the front and back.